Eggstraordinaires

Extraordinary People
Coming out of Their Shells

Elizabeth Goodson and Dion Lucas

TEACH Services, Inc.
PUBLISHING
www.TEACHServices.com • (800) 367-1844

World rights reserved. This book or any portion thereof may not be copied or reproduced in any form or manner whatever, except as provided by law, without the written permission of the publisher, except by a reviewer who may quote brief passages in a review.

The author assumes full responsibility for the accuracy of all facts and quotations as cited in this book. The opinions expressed in this book are the author's personal views and interpretations, and do not necessarily reflect those of the publisher.

This book is provided with the understanding that the publisher is not engaged in giving spiritual, legal, medical, or other professional advice. If authoritative advice is needed, the reader should seek the counsel of a competent professional.

———————————

Copyright © 2020 Elizabeth Goodson and Dion Lucas

Copyright © 2020 TEACH Services, Inc.

ISBN-13: 978-1-4796-1056-3 (Paperback)

ISBN-13: 978-1-4796-1057-0 (ePub)

Table of Contents

Eggstraordinaires 5

Get out of Your Shell! 9

Crack the Egg 11

Boiled Eggs 13

Egg Salad 15

Deviled Eggs 17

Scrambled Eggs 19

Omelets 21

Sunny-Side Up 23

Eggnog 25

Eggstraordinaires...

Enjoy this book as we share some analogies of tasteful egg dishes because people are like eggs in a sense. They can be prepared in so many ways to benefit our society. We, as people, must crack through our shells to cultivate new possibilities, or we risk perishing as rotten eggs.

...continued

Negative influences from media or social groups can impact people's decisions to do harm to self or others. However, there's great joy in knowing there are treatments and resources available to restore people to a healthier state of mind, body, and soul. We all need to be *eggstraordinary*, because we are key ingredients in our world's diverse egg cuisines.

Get out of Your Shell!

A poached egg is an egg that has been cooked outside its shell that can be combined with other ingredients to make a tasteful dish like eggs benedict. However, the analogy of being cooked outside your shell should encourage us all to get out of our comfort zone and broaden our horizons to explore different experiences. America is not the only place that has delightful people and tasteful egg cuisines. We should learn to be comfortable without our "shell"—aka familiar surroundings—and learn to explore different menus—aka cultures and nationalities—because we all know how diverse and delicious other recipes can be. France is known for its delicious quiches. Italy is known for its delightful frittatas, and the flavorful egg burrito is a popular southwestern dish. Overall, the foods we eat should remind us that we, too, can blend in with and respect other cultures to make this world a better place to live.

Crack the Egg

- Break out of Your Shell
- Don't Be Hardheaded
- Open up to New Opportunities

It doesn't matter how you prepare an egg, at some point that egg must come out of its shell in order to be relished and enjoyed. Similarly, everyone must break out of their shell to fulfill their true destiny in life and become *eggstraordinary*.

One thing we can't teach is experience. Experience comes from both good and bad life experiences which we all encounter once we learn to live life outside of our shell. That is why it is so important to listen to trusted adults or mentors who can give you wisdom far beyond what is read in textbooks. After listening to sound council, individuals can proceed in peace because they are doing what they feel is best for themselves and their families. Live life with no fear and regret because you are *eggstraordinary*.

Boiled Eggs

- Take Time to Prepare
- Can Be Soft or Hard
- Gently Crack Open

Working with individuals requires time and patience, which is like boiling eggs. People can be under or overly developed based on their training, but what is defined as a perfect boiled egg depends on a person's perspective. Some people may like individuals who are hard core and very structured, and others may enjoy the company of people who are free spirited with soft hearts that live in the moment from day to day. We all are unique in some form or fashion, which makes this world such a diverse place to live.

Egg Salad

- Needs Cooked Eggs
- Must Have Other Ingredients
- Can Be an Appetizer or Key Dish

An egg salad mix with other ingredients is more tasteful than eating plain boiled eggs. In a sense, diversity can be treated like a tossed egg salad rather than having a mindset of trying to melt people's ideas into one common pot. We all are *eggstraordinary* individuals and no matter our culture or background, we bring flavor to our environment where we can learn to adapt and work together with a good support system.

Deviled Eggs

- Comes from Boiled Eggs
- Unique Presentation
- Extra Seasoning Makes It Divine

Eating a plain boiled egg has great nutritional value, but the appearance is far from eye-catching. Enter the deviled egg! Many TV shows do extreme makeovers on people's appearances to enhance the outer beauty, but the benefit is two-fold. With this exterior change a person also often feels more confident, thus enhancing their inner beauty as well. A new hair style with a nice wardrobe can improve a person's self-esteem and self-worth. We are given one body to cherish throughout our lifetime, and it's important to take proper care of it. Keep life flavorful and jazz it up from time to time!

Scrambled Eggs

- Easy to Make
- Can Be Over or Under Cooked
- Use Seasoning to Increase Taste

Cooking scrambled eggs can be done in either a microwave or skillet to change its texture. This sounds very simple, but it can be difficult to find the perfect balance of cooking and flavor. Even though it's an easy task to prepare a scrambled egg, we shouldn't be caught up in the simple things in life. Everyone needs to apply enough heat to their goal settings to challenge themselves to do greater things for their community and society. So go ahead and accomplish those easy tasks of life but don't forget to spice up your journey with goals that will strengthen your character.

Omelets

- Various Styles
- Uses More Than One Egg
- Tasteful with Other Toppings

Scrambled and fried eggs can be filled with so many ingredients like cheese, chives, onion, peppers, mushrooms, meats, or some combination of the above. Chefs usually prepare tasty omelets with more than just a single egg. Likewise, every successful organization or corporation is built on teamwork from diverse individuals (*eggstraordinaires!*) to use their talents to reach a common goal and be beneficial for the greater good of society. We should learn to mix well with others in order to be more successful in life.

Sunny-Side Up

- Eggs over Easy
- Running Over
- Takes Less Time to Prepare

Having a positive outlook on life is critical to a person's overall health. The characteristics of a sunny-side up egg is what we should abide by. A sunny-side up egg is fried on just one side and can look like the morning sun in the frying pan. Sunshine makes people happy, and the sun is often pictured with a smile on its face. We need to be like that sunny-side up egg! Putting on a smile is easy, it doesn't cost a thing, and it requires less muscles than a frown. We all should want to brighten someone's day with a smile and encouraging words so that it's running over in our homes, schools, and communities. With so much negativity in this world, be the positive change maker and smile!

Eggnog

- Seasonal Drink
- Great to Share Around Holidays
- Used by People of All Ages

Eggnog is a wonderful drink to taste around the winter holidays as we spend time with family and friends to prepare for the upcoming new year. Eggnogs are prepared by combining beaten eggs, cream, and other flavorings. *Eggstraordinaires* are not perfect people, and many times they feel beaten by the world and life experiences. After the beaten eggs are mixed with other ingredients the eggnog is created, and it is a delicious concoction which gives us as humans hope to keep pushing through the beatings of life's challenges. It is encouraging to know we are comforted by others who help keep our life flavorful when we face challenges and know that at the end of the beating you will be better than you were at the start. So, grab that eggnog and toast to a brand new you for breaking out of your shell!

TEACH Services, Inc.
P U B L I S H I N G

We invite you to view the complete
selection of titles we publish at:
www.TEACHServices.com

We encourage you to write us
with your thoughts about this,
or any other book we publish at:
info@TEACHServices.com

TEACH Services' titles may be purchased in
bulk quantities for educational, fund-raising,
business, or promotional use.
bulksales@TEACHServices.com

Finally, if you are interested in seeing
your own book in print, please contact us at:
publishing@TEACHServices.com

We are happy to review your manuscript at no charge.

www.ingramcontent.com/pod-product-compliance
Lightning Source LLC
Chambersburg PA
CBHW061119170426
43200CB00023B/3001